# Advice for parents

The book is designed for children to complete in
but you may like to work with them for the first few pages to check they are happy with reading the questions. They can work through the book unit by unit, or they can dip in and out to practise a particular skill.

The *Practice Workbook* range is easy to use as stand-alone workbooks. They also complement the *Practice* series, which is full of explanations and examples. If your child is finding something tricky, you may like to look at the corresponding *Practice* title to help reinforce and improve their understanding.

## Handwriting

The new National Curriculum for English specifies for Handwriting age 7–9 pupils should be taught to:

- use the horizontal and diagonal strokes, which are needed to join letters and understand which letters, when adjacent to one another, are best left unjoined
- increase the legibility and quality of their handwriting, e.g. by ensuring that the downstrokes of letters are parallel and equidistant; that lines of writing are spaced sufficiently so that the ascenders and descenders of letters do not touch.

When joining letters it is essential that the right joins are used and that writing is regular and well spaced.

The *Practice Workbooks* are more about **visual context** and **motivation** for writing, because good handwriting inevitably comes from an interest in drawing and style. The templates for writing should present situations that encourage children to fill them in.

After each page or section, ask your child, 'Did you enjoy writing it?' 'Would someone else enjoy reading it?' Handwriting is, after all, a means to share thoughts and ideas.

# 1: Letter families

Do you remember the four families of letter shapes?

Write regular lines of each group of letters. Make sure the vertical strokes are parallel.

 **Activity 1**

Long ladder letters start at the top, go down and off in another direction.

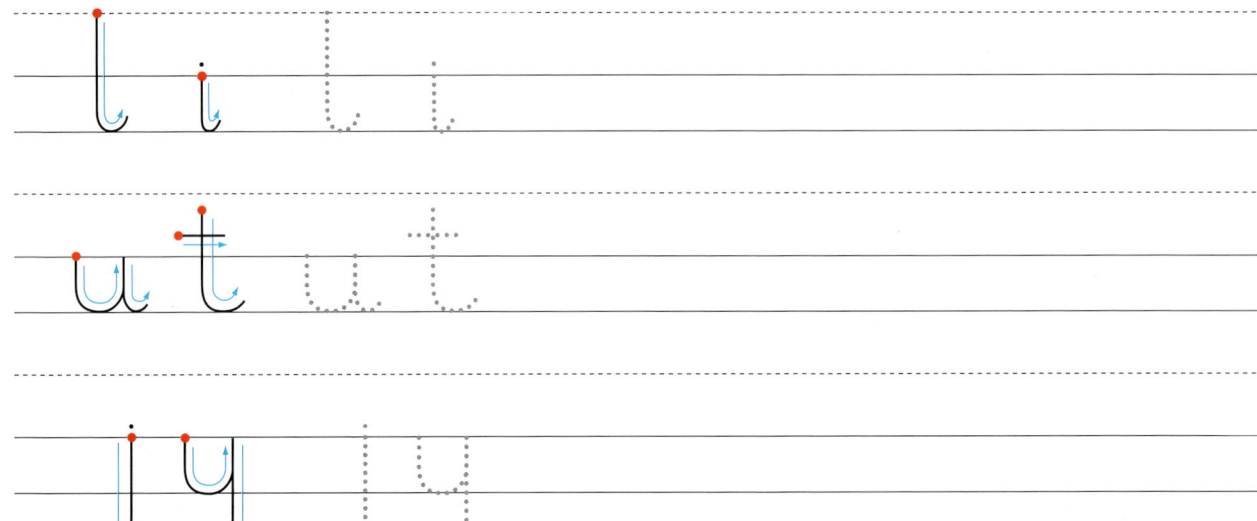

 **Activity 2**

One-armed robot letters start at the top, come down and retrace upwards.

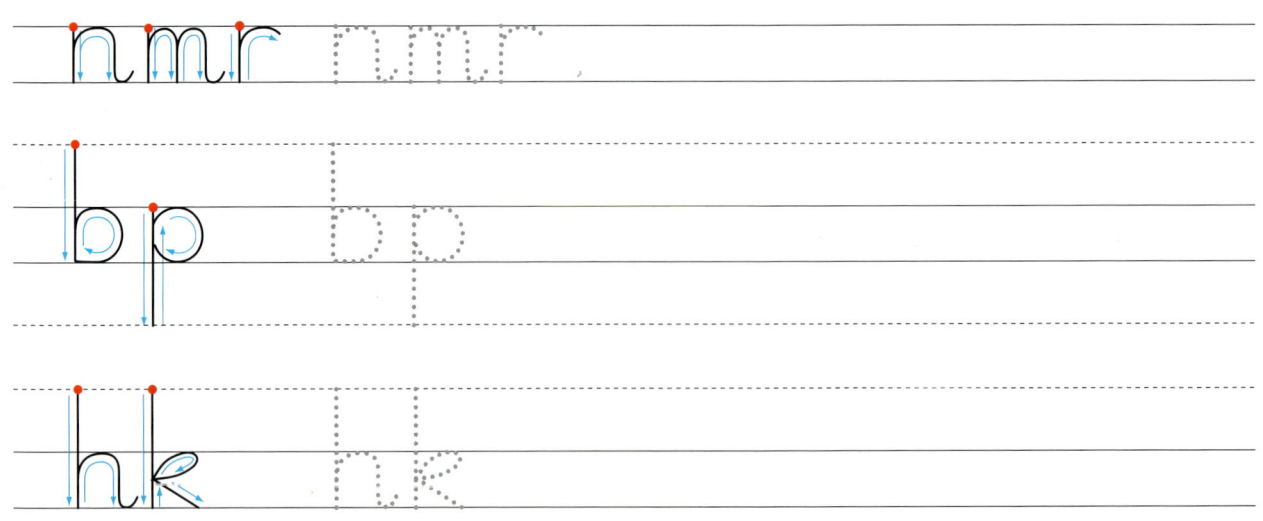

## Activity 3

Curly caterpillar letters curl round in an anticlockwise direction.

o a  o a

c d  c d

s e  s e

f q  f q

o g  o g

## Activity 4

Zigzag letters are all straight lines that change direction.

v w  v w

x z  x z

# 2: The alphabet

**Now practise writing each letter again, this time in the order they come in the alphabet.**

a a A

b b B

c c C

d d D

e e E

f f F

g g G

h h H

i i I

j J

k k K

l l L

# 3: Writing labels

When we write labels, we usually use unjoined print letters. Sometimes we use capital letters and sometimes we use lower case letters.

Fill in these labels. Use the same style as the ones that are already there.

 **Activity 1**

What would you wear to a football match? Draw the clothes, and write labels to explain them, as on pages 8–9.

## Activity 2

What would you wear to a fancy dress party? Draw the clothes, and write labels to explain them.

**Activity 3**

What would you wear to explore the rainforest? Draw the clothes, and write labels to explain them.

## Activity 4

What would you wear to explore Mars? Draw the clothes, and write labels to explain them.

**Activity 5**

What would you wear to meet the Royal Family? Draw the clothes, and write labels to explain them.

**Activity 6**

What would you wear to appear on a TV talent show? Draw the clothes, and write labels to explain them.

# 4: Writing lists

For all these lists use joined writing but not complete sentences.

### Activity 1

You have just been made Prime Minister. What will you do to help the country?

**To Do**

**Activity 2**

You have just been made headteacher. What will you do to help your school?

**To Do**

**Activity 3**

You have won the Lottery. What will you do with the money?

£ _____
£ _____
£ _____
£ _____
£ _____
£ _____
£ _____
£ _____
£ _____
£ _____
£ _____
£ _____
£ _____
£ _____
£ _____
£ _____

**Activity 4**

You have a fortune to give away in your will. To whom will you give it?

£ _____
£ _____
£ _____
£ _____
£ _____
£ _____
£ _____
£ _____
£ _____
£ _____
£ _____
£ _____
£ _____
£ _____
£ _____
£ _____

You are about to sail the Atlantic Ocean. What will you take with you?

**Packing List**

You are about to trek to the North Pole. What will you take with you?

**Packing List**

## Activity 7

You are organising a summer picnic for all your friends. What do you need to buy?

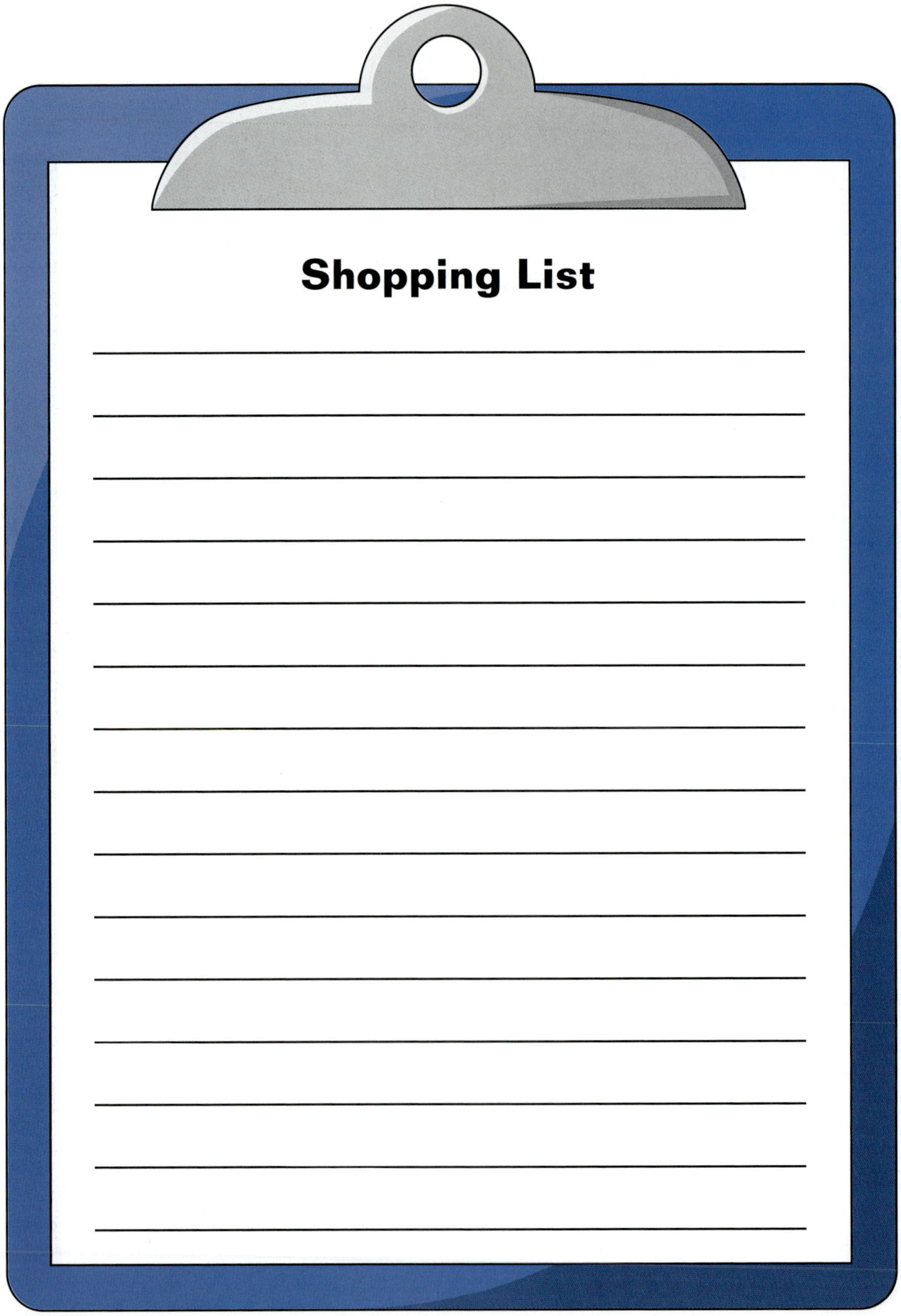
Shopping List

 **Activity 8**

You are organising a party for all your friends. What do you need to buy?

**Shopping List**

# 5: Making joins

Let's revise the five kinds of join, to help you write faster.

The diagonal join is a diagonal line up to the next letter.
Try copying these joins.

ai   ai

un   un

in   in

tr   tr

tw   tw

nm   nm

by   by

dw   dw

## Activity 2

Diagonal joins into ascenders go up into the letters **b**, **f**, **h**, **k**, **l** and **t**.

You have to raise your diagonal line further up, into letters that go above the line.

Try copying these joins.

ab   ab

it   it

eb   eb

ft   ft

sh   sh

il   il

at   at

ib   ib

ul   ul

ch   ch

## Activity 3

For horizontal joins you write a straight line across, from the letters **o**, **r**, **v**, **w** and **f**.

These letters all end at the top, so you just write a straight line across.

Try copying these joins.

ou   ou

wi   wi

on   on

or   or

ov   ov

rw   rw

ri   ri

wr   wr

vi   vi

vw   vw

## Activity 4

Horizontal joins into ascenders go from **o**, **v**, **w**, **r** and **f** into **b**, **f**, **h**, **k**, **l** and **t**.

Your join goes from the top of the small letter up into the tall letter above the line.

Try copying these joins.

# Activity 5

Up and over joins go into the round letters **a**, **c**, **d**, **g**, **o**, **q** and **s**.

Follow the blue arrow to take your pen up and over the next letter, and back down and round.

Try copying these joins.

ta    ta

ac    ac

id    id

eg    eg

ao    ao

uq    uq

is    is

pod   pod

lock  lock

cod cod

lad lad

ice ice

mace mace

mock mock

tab tab

rock rock

flog flog

blood blood

most most

host host

boast boast

**Activity 6**

You don't join at all after the letters **g**, **j**, **y**, **x** and **z**.

You never join after capital letters, either.

Lift your pen after the first letter. Put it back on the second red dot.

ga    ga

je    je

xa    xa

yo    yo

zap   zap

yet   yet

zip   zip

give  give

got   got

jug jug

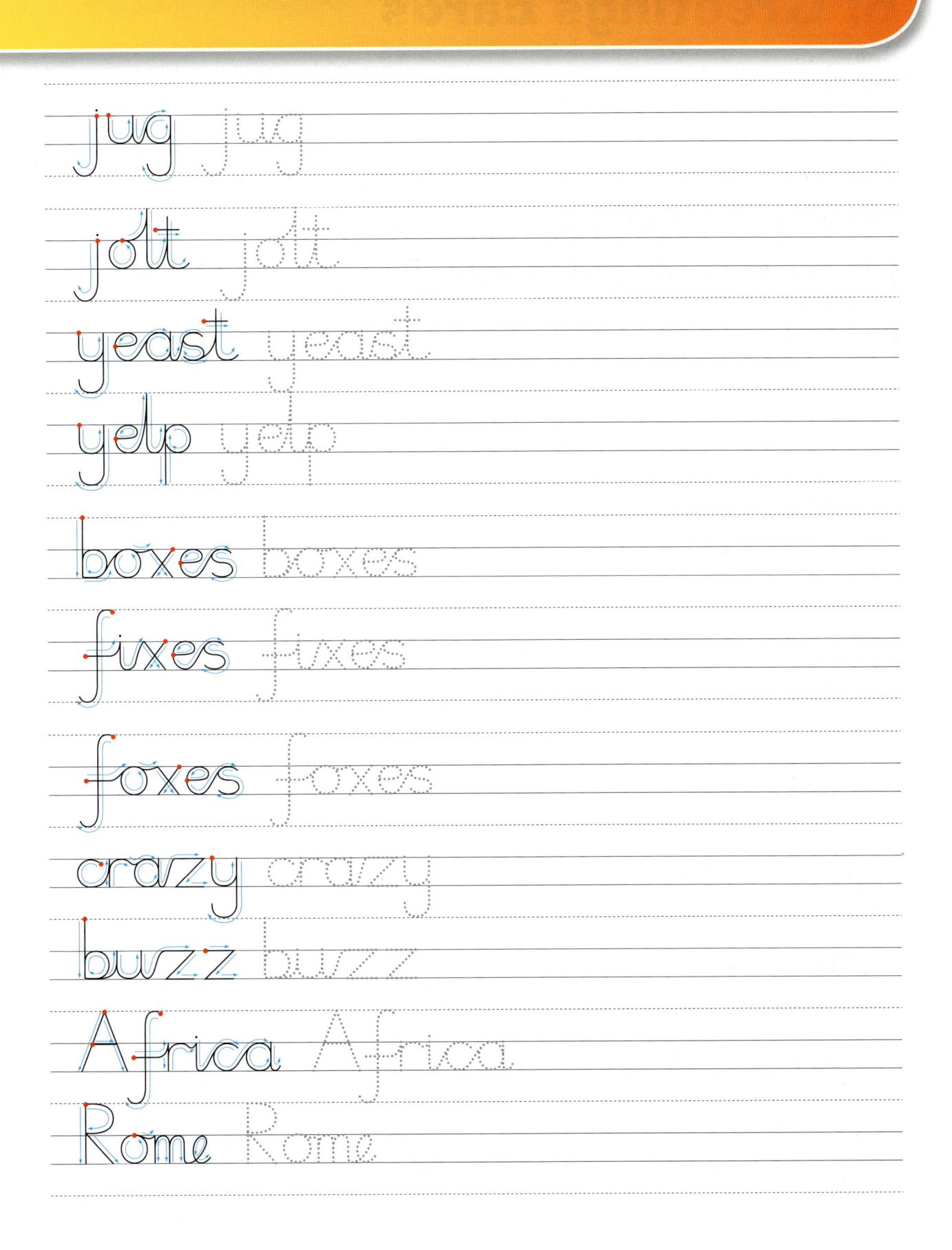

jott jott

yeast yeast

yelp yelp

boxes boxes

fixes fixes

foxes foxes

crazy crazy

buzz buzz

Africa Africa

Rome Rome

# 6: Greetings cards

When you send someone a greetings card, you want to write in your best writing.

## Activity 1

Write a birthday greeting to a friend.

You could hope they have a nice day, and get some good presents!

Remember to say who it's from.

## Activity 2

Maybe someone in your family is going on holiday.

You could wish them a good journey and lots of ice creams!

Remember to say who it's from.

## Activity 3

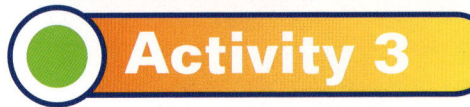

Maybe someone you know has had a new baby.

Send them congratulations!

## Activity 4

Maybe someone you know has passed their exams.

Send them congratulations!

## Activity 5

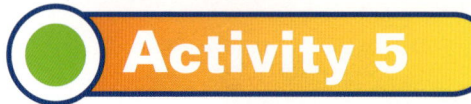

Maybe someone you know has been ill.

Say you hope they'll get better soon.

## Activity 6

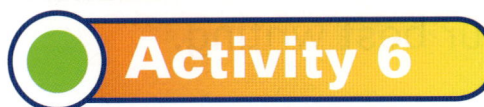

Maybe someone you know is appearing in a show.
Wish them good luck for their big night!

# 7: Writing invitations

With invitations, you want to write in your best writing.

## Activity 1

Your birthday is coming up and you want to invite your friends to a party.

Fill in your invitation on the card and add pictures round the edge.

Would you like to come to my birthday party?

I will be _____ years old.

The date is _____

The time is _____

The address is _____

_____

_____

_____

Please reply to me

_____

### Activity 2

You're going on a bear hunt and you want your friends to come too.

Fill in your invitation on the card and add pictures round the edge.

Would you like to come on a bear hunt?

Time to meet _____

Place to meet _____

_____

Clothes to wear _____

_____

Please bring _____

_____

# Activity 3

You're going to the zoo and you want your friends to come too.

Fill in your invitation on the card and add pictures round the edge.

Would you like to come to the zoo?

Time to meet _____

Place to meet _____

_____

Come dressed as _____

_____

Please bring _____

_____

## Activity 4

You're having a swimming party and you want your friends to come.

Fill in your invitation on the card and add pictures round the edge.

Would you like to come swimming?

Time to meet _____

Place to meet _____
_____

Don't forget _____
_____

Please bring _____
_____

## Activity 5

You're going on a picnic and you want your friends to come too.

Fill in your invitation on the card and add pictures round the edge.

Would you like to come on a picnic?

Time to meet _____

Place to meet _____

_____

Food that I will take _____

_____

Please bring _____

_____

## Activity 6

You're having a barbecue and you want your friends to come round.

Fill in your invitation on the card and add pictures round the edge.

Would you like to come to a barbecue?

Time to meet _____

Place to meet _____
_____

Food at the barbecue _____
_____

Please bring _____
_____

# 8: Writing envelopes

When you're ready to send your greetings cards or your invitations, you need to put them in an envelope.

Envelopes have to be clearly written, so that the postman can read the handwriting.

Here are four real envelopes that did get delivered.

Rewrite each one in your clearest handwriting.

There are no lines for these last few exercises!

## Activity 1

Brenda & Sam
15 Cobden Crescent
Grandpont
Oxford OX1 4LS
England
U.K.

## Activity 2

Delivered by Royal Mail
Royal Mail Cambridge Mail Centre
20.08.12
07:00 pm
13800432

Please remember to write postcode
www.royalm...

Brenda Stones
15, Cobden Crescent
Grandpont
OXFORD OX1.

## Activity 3

THE SOCIETY OF AUTHORS
84 Drayton Gardens SW10 9SB
*The chief glory of every people arises from its authors...*
SAMUEL JOHNSON

LONDON 03.08.12 SW10
GREAT BRITAIN 0044 POSTAGE PAID
PB521868

Brenda Stones
15 Cobden Crescent
Oxford
OX1 4LJ

46

## Activity 4

Brenda Stones
15 Cobden Crescent
OXFORD OX1 4LJ

# 9: Writing postcards

A postcard doesn't give you much space, so you need to write good clear sentences.

Write your message on the left side and the address on the right side.

Then draw a picture of where you've been!

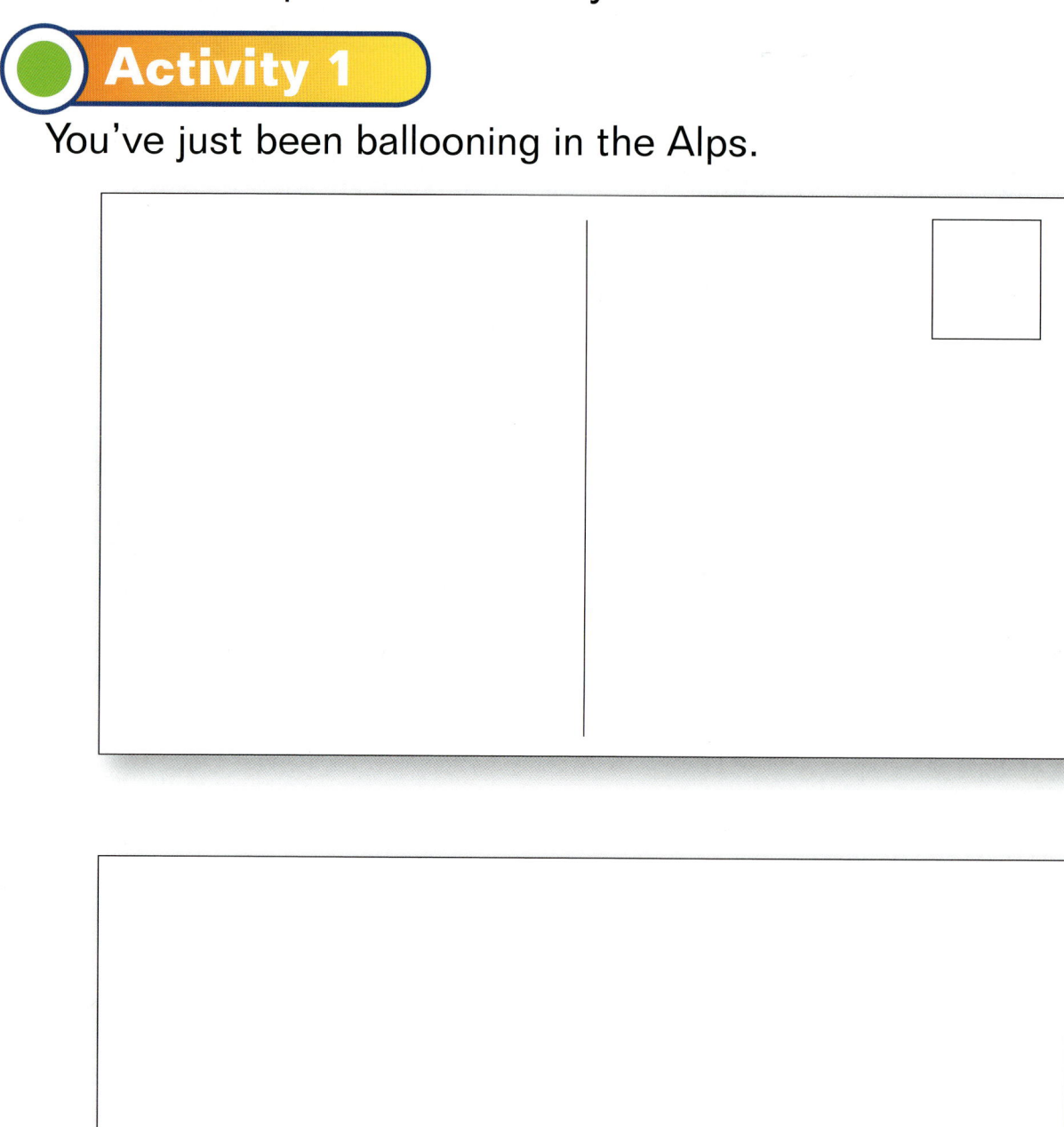

## Activity 1

You've just been ballooning in the Alps.

**Activity 2**

You've just been white-water rafting down the Amazon river.

**Activity 3**

Send this postcard from Antarctica. What did you see?

## Activity 4

You're just back from the Moon. Did you have a good time?

## Activity 5

You've just swum the Channel. You need to tell a few people!

## Activity 6

You've just climbed Mount Everest. Spread the word.

# Activity 7

You've just travelled to a World Cup football match. Tell your friends.

## Activity 8

You've just travelled to an Olympic event. Was it awesome?

# 10: What happened?

Every picture tells a story. Look at the picture and write what might have happened.

## Activity 1

How did the treasure end up on the seabed?

## Activity 2

How did the knights of the castle lose the battle?

_____
_____
_____
_____
_____
_____
_____
_____
_____
_____

**Activity 3**

Who made it to the oasis in the desert?

_____
_____
_____
_____
_____
_____
_____
_____
_____
_____

# Activity 4

Why is there a secret door in the room?

_____
_____
_____
_____
_____
_____
_____
_____
_____
_____
_____
_____

## Activity 5

Why did the plane land in the jungle?

_____
_____
_____
_____
_____
_____
_____
_____
_____
_____
_____
_____
_____

**Activity 6**

Why was the house abandoned?

_____
_____
_____
_____
_____
_____
_____
_____
_____
_____
_____
_____

## Activity 7

Who was unable to use their car?

_____
_____
_____
_____
_____
_____
_____
_____
_____
_____
_____
_____

**Activity 8**

What happened to the wearer of the magic ring?

_____
_____
_____
_____
_____
_____
_____
_____
_____
_____
_____
_____

# The UK's biggest home-learning range

**WHSmith**

These **WHSmith English Practice Workbooks** are available for **ages 7–11**

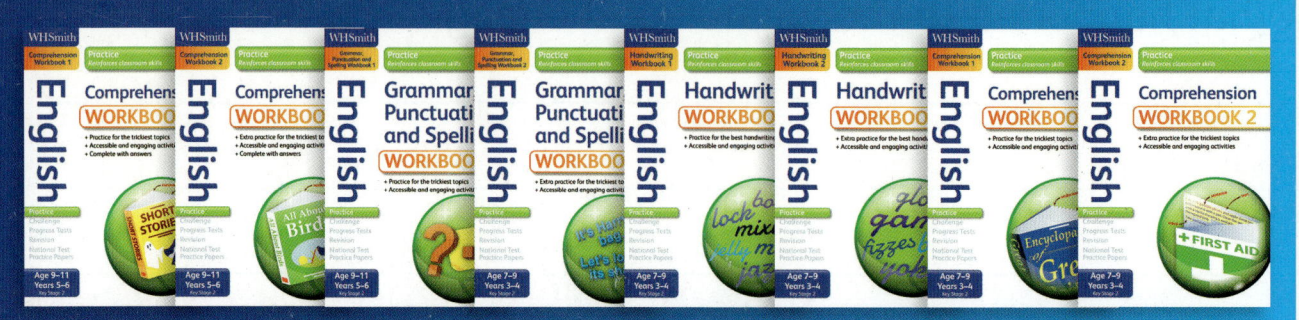

Maths titles are also available.

## Your Learning Journey

The comprehensive range of **WHSmith** home-learning books forms a Learning Journey that supports children's education and helps to prepare for every success at school. We support children – and parents – through every step of that journey.

- **Practice** – Reinforces classroom core skills
- **Challenge** – Stretches more-able children
- **Progress** – 10-minute progress checks
- **Revision** – Develop skills for tests
- **Test** – Practice for National Tests

## Practice

The **WHSmith Practice Workbooks** for key stage 2 provide extra activities and support, building your child's confidence and understanding.

+ Plenty of practice to boost confidence
+ Builds handwriting skills
+ More fun activities for you to work through at home
+ Written by experienced teachers

For more information plus advice and support for parents visit
www.whsmith.co.uk/readytoprogress

Shop online at whsmith.co.uk
WH Smith Retail Ltd SN3 3RX

ISBN 978-1-4441-8874-5